"THERE IS NO GREATER AGONY THAN BEARING AN UNTOLD STORY INSIDE YOU."

—MAYA ANGELOU, *I KNOW WHY THE CAGED BIRD SINGS*

> *"THE ONLY WAY OUT OF THE LABYRINTH*
> *OF SUFFERING IS TO FORGIVE."*
> —JOHN GREEN, *LOOKING FOR ALASKA*

> **"THE WORLD, EVEN THE SMALLEST PARTS OF IT, IS FILLED WITH THINGS YOU DON'T KNOW."**
> —SHERMAN ALEXIE, *THE ABSOLUTELY TRUE DIARY OF A PART-TIME INDIAN*

> *"WE CAN'T TAKE ANY CREDIT FOR OUR TALENTS.*
> *IT'S HOW WE USE THEM THAT COUNTS."*
>
> —MADELEINE L'ENGLE, *A WRINKLE IN TIME*

> *"LOVE WHO YOU WANT TO LOVE, AND DO IT UNAPOLOGETICALLY, INCLUDING THAT FACE YOU SEE EVERY DAY IN THE MIRROR."*
>
> —GEORGE M. JOHNSON, *ALL BOYS AREN'T BLUE*

"I WAS WITHIN AND WITHOUT, SIMULTANEOUSLY ENCHANTED AND REPELLED BY THE INEXHAUSTIBLE VARIETY OF LIFE."

—F. SCOTT FITZGERALD, *THE GREAT GATSBY*

> **"WORDS CAN BE LIKE X-RAYS IF YOU USE THEM PROPERLY—THEY'LL GO THROUGH ANYTHING. YOU READ AND YOU'RE PIERCED."**
> —ALDOUS HUXLEY, *BRAVE NEW WORLD*

> ## "WHAT STICKS TO MEMORY, OFTEN, ARE THOSE ODD LITTLE FRAGMENTS THAT HAVE NO BEGINNING AND NO END..."
>
> —TIM O'BRIEN, *THE THINGS THEY CARRIED*

> *"WHEN WE THINK OF THE PAST IT'S THE BEAUTIFUL THINGS WE PICK OUT. WE WANT TO BELIEVE IT WAS ALL LIKE THAT."*
>
> —MARGARET ATWOOD, *THE HANDMAID'S TALE*

> ## "BETWEEN THE OCEAN AND THE MOUNTAINS IS A WILD FOREST. THAT IS WHERE I WANT TO MAKE MY HOME."
> —MAIA KOBABE, *GENDER QUEER: A MEMOIR*

"PEOPLE GENERALLY SEE WHAT THEY LOOK FOR, AND HEAR WHAT THEY LISTEN FOR..."

—HARPER LEE, *TO KILL A MOCKINGBIRD*

**"MAN, WHEN YOU LOSE YOUR LAUGH
YOU LOSE YOUR FOOTING."**

—KEN KESEY, *ONE FLEW OVER THE CUCKOO'S NEST*

> *"MAYBE THE TWO DIFFERENT WORLDS WE LIVED IN*
> *WEREN'T SO DIFFERENT. WE SAW THE SAME SUNSET."*
>
> —S.E. HINTON, *THE OUTSIDERS*

> *"I WISH I COULD FREEZE THIS MOMENT, RIGHT HERE,*
> *RIGHT NOW AND LIVE IN IT FOREVER."*
> —SUZANNE COLLINS, *THE HUNGER GAMES: CATCHING FIRE*

"... IT'S THE LITTLE THINGS THAT SMOOTHES PEOPLE'S ROADS THE MOST..."

—MARK TWAIN, *THE ADVENTURES OF HUCKLEBERRY FINN*

"HE WAS GOING TO LIVE FOREVER, OR DIE IN THE ATTEMPT."
—JOSEPH HELLER, *CATCH-22*

"'YOU HAVE BEEN MY FRIEND,' REPLIED CHARLOTTE.
'THAT IN ITSELF IS A TREMENDOUS THING.'"

—E.B. WHITE, *CHARLOTTE'S WEB*

> *"PERHAPS I'VE SPENT TOO LONG IN THE COMPANY OF MY LITERARY ROMANTIC HEROES, AND CONSEQUENTLY MY IDEALS AND EXPECTATIONS ARE FAR TOO HIGH."*
>
> —E.L. JAMES, *FIFTY SHADES OF GREY*

"NO ONE KNOWS FOR CERTAIN HOW MUCH IMPACT THEY HAVE ON THE LIVES OF OTHER PEOPLE."

—JAY ASHER, *THIRTEEN REASONS WHY*

"IF HAPPINESS IS ANTICIPATION WITH CERTAINTY, WE WERE HAPPY."

—TONI MORRISON, *THE BLUEST EYE*

**"'ALL SHALL BE DONE,' SAID ASLAN.
'BUT IT MAY BE HARDER THAN YOU THINK.'"**

—C.S. LEWIS, *THE LION, THE WITCH, AND THE WARDROBE*

> *"THE WOUND BEGINS TO CLOSE IN ON ITSELF, TO PROTECT WHAT IS HURTING SO MUCH. AND ONCE IT IS CLOSED, YOU NO LONGER SEE WHAT IS UNDERNEATH, WHAT STARTED THE PAIN."*
>
> —AMY TAN, *THE JOY LUCK CLUB*

"THERE SHOULD BE A PLACE WHERE ONLY THE THINGS YOU WANT TO HAPPEN, HAPPEN."

—MAURICE SENDAK, *WHERE THE WILD THINGS ARE*

> *"...IF PEOPLE AREN'T ALLOWED TO SAY WHAT'S REALLY ON THEIR MINDS FOR FEAR OF UPSETTING PEOPLE, WE'LL END UP NEVER SAYING ANYTHING AT ALL."*
>
> —JUNO DAWSON, *THIS BOOK IS GAY*

> ## "SOMETIMES IT HELPS TO SCOLD YOURSELF,
> ## TO GIVE YOURSELF ADVICE."
>
> —R.L. STINE, *GOOSEBUMPS: THE HAUNTED MASK II*

**"'MY DEAR YOUNG FELLOW,' THE OLD-GREEN-GRASSHOPPER
SAID GENTLY, 'THERE ARE A WHOLE LOT OF THINGS IN THIS WORLD
OF OURS YOU HAVEN'T STARTED WONDERING ABOUT YET.'"**

—ROALD DAHL, *JAMES AND THE GIANT PEACH*

> *"IT WAS UP TO HIM TO PAY BACK TO THE WORLD IN BEAUTY AND CARING WHAT LESLIE HAD LOANED HIM IN VISION AND STRENGTH."*
>
> —KATHERINE PATERSON, *BRIDGE TO TERABITHIA*

> *"THE MARK OF THE IMMATURE MAN IS THAT HE WANTS TO DIE NOBLY FOR A CAUSE, WHILE THE MARK OF THE MATURE MAN IS THAT HE WANTS TO LIVE HUMBLY FOR ONE."*
>
> —J.D. SALINGER, *THE CATCHER IN THE RYE*

> *"I FELT MY LUNGS INFLATE WITH THE ONRUSH OF SCENERY—AIR, MOUNTAINS, TREES, PEOPLE. I THOUGHT, 'THIS IS WHAT IT IS TO BE HAPPY.'"*
>
> —SYLVIA PLATH, *THE BELL JAR*

**"IT'S THE JOB THAT'S NEVER STARTED
AS TAKES LONGEST TO FINISH..."**
—J.R.R. TOLKIEN, *THE LORD OF THE RINGS: THE FELLOWSHIP OF THE RING*

"...ALL HUMAN WISDOM IS CONTAINED
IN THESE TWO WORDS—WAIT AND HOPE."

—ALEXANDRE DUMAS, *THE COUNT OF MONTE CRISTO*

> *"THE WORST PART OF HOLDING THE MEMORIES*
> *IS NOT THE PAIN. IT'S THE LONELINESS OF IT.*
> *MEMORIES NEED TO BE SHARED."*
> —LOIS LOWRY, *THE GIVER*

"PERHAPS IT IS BETTER TO WAKE UP AFTER ALL, EVEN TO SUFFER, RATHER THAN TO REMAIN A DUPE TO ILLUSIONS ALL ONE'S LIFE."

—KATE CHOPIN, *THE AWAKENING*

> *"SOMETIMES THE DREAMS THAT COME TRUE ARE THE DREAMS YOU NEVER EVEN KNEW YOU HAD."*
>
> —ALICE SEBOLD, *THE LOVELY BONES*

"BRAVE DOESN'T MEAN YOU'RE NOT SCARED.
IT MEANS YOU GO ON EVEN THOUGH YOU'RE SCARED."

—ANGIE THOMAS, *THE HATE U GIVE*

"BELIEVING TAKES PRACTICE."

—MADELEINE L'ENGLE, *A WIND IN THE DOOR*

"BUT WHERE THERE'S HOPE, THERE'S LIFE. IT FILLS US WITH FRESH COURAGE AND MAKES US STRONG AGAIN."

—ANNE FRANK, *THE DIARY OF A YOUNG GIRL*

*"THOSE DEFICITS, THEY MAKE US REACH, THEY STRETCH US.
THEY MAKE US FIGHT BACK WHEN IT MATTERS."*

—JONATHAN EVISON, *LAWN BOY*

> *"ONE BENEFIT OF SUMMER WAS THAT EACH DAY WE HAD MORE LIGHT TO READ BY."*
>
> —JEANNETTE WALLS, *THE GLASS CASTLE*

"TO THE STARS WHO LISTEN—AND THE DREAMS THAT ARE ANSWERED."

—SARAH J. MAAS, *A COURT OF MIST AND FURY*

> *"FREEING YOURSELF WAS ONE THING, CLAIMING OWNERSHIP OF THAT FREED SELF WAS ANOTHER."*
>
> —TONI MORRISON, *BELOVED*

*"TO DIE, IT'S EASY...BUT YOU HAVE
TO STRUGGLE FOR LIFE."*
—ART SPIEGELMAN, *MAUS*

"YOU CAN'T GET AWAY FROM YOURSELF BY MOVING FROM ONE PLACE TO ANOTHER."

—ERNEST HEMINGWAY, *THE SUN ALSO RISES*

"IT IS OUR CHOICES, HARRY, THAT SHOW WHAT WE TRULY ARE, FAR MORE THAN OUR ABILITIES."

—J.K. ROWLING, *HARRY POTTER AND THE CHAMBER OF SECRETS*

"IF THERE'S GOT TO BE A FUTURE FOR HUMANITY, THERE'LL HAVE TO BE A VERY BIG CHANGE FROM WHAT NOW IS."

—D.H. LAWRENCE, *LADY CHATTERLEY'S LOVER*

> *"IT IS TO THE CREDIT OF HUMAN NATURE, THAT,
> EXCEPT WHERE ITS SELFISHNESS IS BROUGHT INTO PLAY,
> IT LOVES MORE READILY THAN IT HATES."*
>
> —NATHANIEL HAWTHORNE, *THE SCARLET LETTER*

*"IT TAKES TEN TIMES AS LONG TO PUT YOURSELF
BACK TOGETHER AS IT DOES TO FALL APART."*

—SUZANNE COLLINS, *THE HUNGER GAMES: MOCKINGJAY*

"'STUFF YOUR EYES WITH WONDER,' HE SAID, 'LIVE AS IF YOU'D DROP DEAD IN TEN SECONDS. SEE THE WORLD. IT'S MORE FANTASTIC THAN ANY DREAM MADE OR PAID FOR IN FACTORIES.'"

—RAY BRADBURY, *FAHRENHEIT 451*

"EVEN STRENGTH MUST BOW TO WISDOM SOMETIMES."
—RICK RIORDAN, *PERCY JACKSON AND THE OLYMPIANS: THE LIGHTNING THIEF*

> *"IT MAY BE UNFAIR, BUT WHAT HAPPENS IN A FEW DAYS, SOMETIMES EVEN A SINGLE DAY, CAN CHANGE THE COURSE OF A WHOLE LIFETIME..."*
> —KHALED HOSSEINI, *THE KITE RUNNER*

> *"WHEN PEOPLE DON'T EXPRESS THEMSELVES,*
> *THEY DIE ONE PIECE AT A TIME."*
> —LAURIE HALSE ANDERSON, *SPEAK*

> **"ALL ANIMALS ARE EQUAL, BUT SOME ANIMALS ARE MORE EQUAL THAN OTHERS."**
> —GEORGE ORWELL, *ANIMAL FARM*

> *"I THINK US HERE TO WONDER, MYSELF. TO WONDER. TO ASK. AND THAT IN WONDERING BOUT THE BIG THINGS AND ASKING BOUT THE BIG THINGS, YOU LEARN ABOUT THE LITTLE ONES, ALMOST BY ACCIDENT."*
>
> —ALICE WALKER, *THE COLOR PURPLE*

> *"THE THING IS—FEAR CAN'T HURT YOU*
> *ANY MORE THAN A DREAM."*
> —WILLIAM GOLDING, *LORD OF THE FLIES*

"AND IN THAT MOMENT, I SWEAR WE WERE INFINITE."

—STEPHEN CHBOSKY, *THE PERKS OF BEING A WALLFLOWER*

"ONE THING I'VE LEARNED ABOUT PEOPLE IS THAT THE EASIEST WAY TO GET THEM TO LIKE YOU IS TO SHUT UP AND LET THEM DO THE TALKING."

—JESSE ANDREWS, *ME AND EARL AND THE DYING GIRL*

"THERE IS AN ECSTASY THAT MARKS THE SUMMIT OF LIFE, AND BEYOND WHICH LIFE CANNOT RISE."

—JACK LONDON, *THE CALL OF THE WILD*

> *"UNTIL I FEARED I WOULD LOSE IT, I NEVER LOVED TO READ. ONE DOES NOT LOVE BREATHING."*
>
> —HARPER LEE, *TO KILL A MOCKINGBIRD*

"PATIENCE IS A CONQUERING VIRTUE."

—GEOFFREY CHAUCER, *THE CANTERBURY TALES*

> ## "ALL WE HAVE TO DECIDE IS WHAT TO DO WITH THE TIME THAT IS GIVEN US."
>
> —J.R.R. TOLKIEN, *THE LORD OF THE RINGS: THE FELLOWSHIP OF THE RING*

**"PERHAPS ONE DID NOT WANT TO BE LOVED
SO MUCH AS TO BE UNDERSTOOD."**

—GEORGE ORWELL, *1984*

*"HERE WE ARE, ALIVE, AND YOU AND I
WILL HAVE TO MAKE IT WHAT WE CAN."*
—GERALDINE BROOKS, *YEAR OF WONDERS*

"OF COURSE THEY NEEDED TO CARE. IT WAS THE MEANING OF EVERYTHING."

—LOIS LOWRY, *THE GIVER*

*"DID MY HEART LOVE TILL NOW? FORSWEAR IT, SIGHT!
FOR I NE'ER SAW TRUE BEAUTY TILL THIS NIGHT."*

—WILLIAM SHAKESPEARE, *ROMEO AND JULIET*

"IT DOES NOT DO WELL TO DWELL ON DREAMS AND FORGET TO LIVE, REMEMBER THAT."

—J.K. ROWLING, *HARRY POTTER AND THE SORCERER'S STONE*